HAITIAN CREOLE CHILDREN'S BOOK

The Wonderful Wizard of Oz

WAI CHEUNG

©Copyright, 2017, by Wai Cheung and Maestro Publishing Group
All rights reserved.

No part of this book may be reproduced or transmitted in any form or by any means, electronic or mechanical, including photocopying, recording or by any information storage and retrieval system, without permission in writing of the copyright owner.

Printed in the United States of America.

ABOUT THE BOOK

Raise your children in a bilingual fashion with this bilingual coloring book that captures the magic and beauty of Wizard of Oz's story along with a dual language storytelling that is perfect for parents who want to raise their children in a bilingual environment.

CONTENTS

Plate 1 3

Plate 2 5

Plate 3 7

Plate 4 9

Plate 5 11

Plate 6 13

Plate 7 15

Plate 8 17

This page intentionally left blank.

Dorothy Gale, who lived in Kansas with her Uncle Henry, Aunt Em and her little dog Toto, found herself nearly swept away by a large tornado.

Dorothy Gale ki te viv lavil Kansas ansanm ak Tonton Henry, Matant Em epi ti chyen li Toto. Yon gwo tonton van tanpèt manke bote Dorothy Gale ale.

Plate 1

The tornado picked up the entire house with Dorothy and Toto in it and deposited them in a land where Munchkins greeted them with joy.

Gwo van tanpèt la te bwote tout kay la ansanm ak tout Dorothy ak Toto ladan l, apresa li te depoze yo sou yon tèren kote Munchkins salye yo ak kè kontan.

Plate 2

The Good Witch of the North told Dorothy that in order to return home, she must see the Wizard of Oz in the Emerald City, and she gave the girl a pair of magical Silver Shoes.

Sòsye Bon Bagay Nò a te di Dorothy ke li dwe wè Majisyen Bèl Mèvèy Oz la ki nan Vil Emeral la si li vle tounen lakay li, epi li te ba li jenn tifi a yon Soulye majik annò.

Plate 3

Along the way, Dorothy met three new friends: The Scarecrow, The Tin Woodman and the Cowardly Lion.

Sou wout la, Dorothy kontre ak twa nouvo zanmi : Epouvantay, Koupèd Bwa, ak Lyon Kapon

Plate 4

Dorothy and her new friends made it to the Emerald City, where the Wizard gave them all the same mission: Destroy the Wicked Witch of the West.

Dorothy ak nouvo zanmi li yo te rive nan Lavil Emeral la, kote Majisyen a te ba yo menm misyon : pou touye Sòsye Mechan Lwès la.

Plate 5

The Wicked Witch finally captured Dorothy and made her a personal slave, all while attempting to steal the Silver Shoes.

Sòsye Mechan an te finalman trape Dorothy epi te fè li tounen esklav, tout sa pandan lap chache vòlò Soulye annò yo.

Plate 6

The Wicked Witch got one shoe from Dorothy, but the young girl became so angry she picked up the bucket and tossed the water on the witch — who, to her surprise, melted!

Sòsye Mechan an te pran yon soulye nan men Dorothy, men jenn tifi a te vin tèlman fache, li pran bokit la, voye dlo a sou Sòsye a – li te sezi wè Sòsye a fonn tankou yon glas!

Plate 7

Jubilant, Dorothy and her friends returned to the Emerald City, and Glinda, the Good Witch of the South, showed her how to return to Kansas: click her heels together three times and wish for home.

Ak kè kontan, Dorothy ak zanmi li yo retounen al nan Lavil Emeral la, epi Glinda, Sòsye Bon Bagay Sid la, te montre li kijan pou li retounen lavil Kansas : frape talon pye l yo ansanm twa fwa epi panse ak lakay.

Plate 8

This page intentionally left blank.

ABOUT THE BOOK

Raise your children in a bilingual fashion with this bilingual coloring book that captures the magic and beauty of Wizard of Oz's story along with a dual language storytelling that is perfect for parents who want to raise their children in a bilingual environment.

Made in United States
Orlando, FL
19 May 2023